Don Savant's

Book of Poems, Sonnets and Vows for Relationships and Weddings

PublishAmerica
Baltimore

ISBN: 1-60672-215-8
PUBLISHED BY PUBLISHAMERICA, LLLP
www.publishamerica.com
Baltimore

Printed in the United States of America

Dedication

To D.E.W.:

I don't know you well, but I thank you regardless. It took a complete stranger to open my eyes to my life's purpose. It'd been there all the time and it's because of you that I finally recognize what it is that I'm supposed to use this gift for. For that I thank you, my sister in God.

Dear Reader,

What is love? It's become evident that no one knows the true definition in this day in time. Love used to be beautiful; it used to be natural, with a certain amount of spiritual sacredness to it. I'll tell you what the biggest factor of love is. God. Think about it, God is love. Therefore, without God, you cannot truly experience love as it was meant to be. If you think otherwise, then you have definitely fallen short of truly knowing and identifying with one of life's greatest gifts.

I feel that it is my duty to bring love back to the world through my poetry. Anyone that is in a relationship that is lacking, or is in a marriage that has lost something, this is the book for you. If you are about to say your vows, and can't find the exact words that you'd like to say, allow me to say them for you. I have put this book together for anyone seeking to find love. No matter if you are single, married, engaged, or otherwise, if you are searching for the perfect words for the perfect moments in your relationships, look no further. It's time to bring love back. I'll be your guide. Thank you for reading. Apply at will.

—Don Savant

Table of Contents

The Vow

as i stand before you
i now know that
my search is finally over
because in you
i've found
everything that
i've ever wanted and needed in a woman

as you stand before me
i can barely contain
and compose myself
and i'm holding back both tears of joy
and the biggest smile
that any man has ever smiled before

i thank you
i thank God
for helping turn you and i
into us
and allowing me to share this moment
with one of the many Angels
that He sent to roam this earth

the forever that stands before us
is patiently waiting

for us to shine
and to set an example to those
who no longer believe in
the truth of love

you are mine and
i am yours
from now
until we both rest eternally

Real Love

at night...

when i lay beside you...

i can feel your pulse running through me and

slo-w-ly...

i can feel myself...

falling in love with you...

i guess it's no...

coincidence that...

we became us...

not based off of lust but...

something deeper

that was placed within...

that we both sought after and found...

at exactly the right moment in our lives...

and with you i rise...

to every occasion...

showing you...

the definition of a real man...

a real king...

representing his queen and...

resurrecting the faith

that you once had in mankind

there is nothing subliminal about us...

simply because we trust...

one another with the truth...

and with that...

we are free...

free to be...

who we are...

to live as us...

in all our blessed splendor

while not losing our separate identities...

you are the...future bearer of my last name...

the...

future garden...

playing host to my seed...

which i intend to plant

ever so graciously...

with a halo of love surrounding us as you nurture...

and our sons and daughters

grow inside of you...

to be presented to this world...

under the wings of you and i...

committed...

forever remaining in tact...

for both their sake...

ours...

and those who wish to have

what we display

every hour...

of each

and every day...

never will i...

ever find...

what lies within you...

and i'll never do...

anything...

to decimate this family circle...

centered by God Himself to give stability to...

the real definition...

of what a man and woman

are really supposed to be

The L Word

the power of your smile

blinded by her beauty
as her hips move from side to side
seeming to be
in slow motion
every time she walks by

continues to

i can't seem to
get enough of
that smile that
hides behind her full lips and
that voice that
shakes the internal foundation of me

make me realize

my thought process
is severely bruised
not from abuse but
from the
countless number of times
each moment

of each day
when the contents of your beautiful soul
lay across my temporal lobes

just how much

a constant
warm chill runs through me
as if my
blood consists of
icy hot
because i know that
you'll always
share a part of my vitality

i love you

the cracks in my heart
have been healed
and sealed by you
completing me in a way that
i've never known before now
you have
shown me that
my tears
and my emotions
are the things that
make me a man

your man

and that

anyone that thinks any less of me

must not know

just how powerful

the L word can be

every day that we're together

Love in A-Minor

i have a song
deep within my heart
whose lyrics are
still unfinished
and whose rhythm is
offset by
the constant changes
in the pattern of my heartbeat

my melody
has no accompaniment
as there is no hook
to bring together my verses

i have no harmony
therefore
i'm a walking acapella
unmixed and unmastered
just a mere concept
with no one to follow me through
until my production is complete

Unexpected

the little time that i've spent with you has been
the greatest moments of my life and
this is exactly what i've always searched for

and i can tell you right now that
all of the things that i thought to be true have
gone far away from my thought process

only the two of us have these memories
that will last within both of us for an eternity

and at last i know what true love really feels like and
i can see past my own selfish ways and
it is such an eye opening change
because of the alterations you placed on my heart making my
troubles with past relationships cease to matter anymore

you are the golden ray of sunshine in my life
you are the epitome of God's best work
you are the one who i need in my world
what else could this be but a magnetic attraction
it is perfectly pulling us together in ways i've never imagined
you are…nothing less than perfection
what more could any man want in this life

strange, how the unexpected always finds the light of day

My Girl

you are
poetic perfection
in every way possible

each verse
represents
a different part of you

each line
exposes your depth
in more ways
than anyone
could ever imagine…

i write
to your heartbeat…
because
that rhythm within you
soothes my pen and
causes it to
glide smoothly across this notepad
spelling out
the true definition of you
from your first stanza(head)
to your last(toe)

your story
has been told before but
the details have
never been so clear
and the moral
has never held more meaning

you are the lyrics
to the song that
only plays for me and
i hope to have you on repeat
for the rest of my days

Transparency

my love
is the deepest part of me
it is
why i am
who i am

the love within me
is unconditional
it is limitless
with no boundaries to hold it back

my emotions are strong
so much that
anyone that doesn't know me
may mistake me
for less than a man
but my ability
to show what i feel
makes me even more
simply because
i'm not afraid
to show my true colors

when i love you
it's so undeniable that

you'll know
before i even tell you
because i'll show you
before you even have a clue

i'll show you
everything
that lies within my soul
and i'll be
everything you need me to be

that's
what i'm all about…
that…emotion
that urgent sense of commitment
that
brand new reason
every single day to stand back and say
i love you
that gets deeper
and deeper
every time we exchange whispers

let me be
transparent for you
while i
give you something you've never expected
every day that you're mine

More than a Woman

words cannot explain
nor can
any sentiment that i display
relay to you
just how beautiful
i think you are

i'm not speaking of
physical beauty
even though
your eyes
your lips
and everything else featured on
that fantastic body of yours is
nothing short of amazing but
aside from that
everything within you is
more than immaculate

your personality...
your drive...
your focus...
makes me want to strive
to be more than what i am
with you
leading by example

when i fell for you
it was soul first...
because to be honest
i looked at you
from the inside out
i mean...
yes, i noticed your attractiveness
but with most ladies
that's where the goodness starts and ends but
something in my gut told me
"she's different"
and i found that
there's never been
truer words spoken
and i stand here
with tears streaming down both cheeks
so happy that i listened
to that voice
that sent me in your direction

you are
the only thing in this world
that could make perfection nervous
because you are more than
the total package
that real men seek to find
you are

God's crowning achievement

as well as

my Angel on this earth

Reminiscence

your sensuous gaze
reminds me of
a love that i once captured
and a love that i once lost
that stare…those
beautiful eyes set into that
beautiful face that
was composed of
such beautiful skin that
curved around those
beautiful lips from which
the voice of an angel escaped
with each word that she spoke

having you near me
makes me reminisce…makes me
glad that i went through those things with her
because they brought me to you and
it reminds me that
love is not dead in me

The Rhythm of Your Heart

when i close my eyes
i can hear your heart beat
and the music…
the rhythm…
that it makes
soothes me subtly
it…
makes me want
you…
to comfort you
to be here
with you
and for you
from this moment
until
your song
stops playing for me

The Music of Our Hearts

let me take your hand
and dance with you
to the music of our hearts
to the music of our hearts
to the music of our hearts
to the music of our...
forgive me
but when i'm near you
my heart skips a beat
and i...
well honestly
i want to spend an eternity
in this moment
wrapped up in your arms
singing in your ear
everything that comes to mind
while
creating memories
that we'll share
until our song plays no more

The Promise

can i

walk you through my mind

for just a moment

to show you

instead of

telling you

what emotions unfold within me

when you're on my brain

if you had

some understanding of

what makes me

who i am and

what makes me

love you like i do and

want you like i do then

you'd fully understand me as a man

as

your man

your king

and hopefully

the last man

you'll ever allow yourself to love

i want you to

see for yourself

the sacrifices that
i'm willing to make for you
and how
together
we can accomplish so much in this life

we can be
the example
that shows everyone that
love is still real
and it still exists in the hearts and minds of many
that are afraid to
let it be known

we can show the world that
love does not equate to fear
and our actions will solidify
what we already know to be true

explore me
thoroughly
and learn my inner workings
and let us stand together
as a united front
you portraying love
me portraying happiness
and us
portraying the promise that God made
when He placed you by my side

Where We Belong

my present
and my future
stands before me right now
making my past
completely irrelevant

this moment
before you...
our families and friends
and before God
is what i've been waiting for
ever since the day
that i realized
the definition of true love

i arise each morning
with you in my heart
and your soul
occupies my body
making me
more complete
than i've ever been
in this journey we call life

everything you do for me

i want to do

tenfold

to show my undying devotion to you

we will walk together

in unison

not one in front of

or behind the other

but

right beside each other

where we both belong

on this day

and all that follow

under the umbrella of peace

love

and happiness

that has been provided by God

The Essence of My Love

when i love
i love strong
i love
completely
without a doubt
without…
uncertainty…

i love
with the entire contents
of my heart and
i make sure that
she is satisfied
beyond her wildest dreams
i make sure that
i am the man that
does things for her
in ways that
no other man before me has and
in the event that
we don't last forever i
reach levels of her heart that
no man that
comes after me will ever be able to attain

i spoil
with my touch and
with my kisses and
with my words and
well…
lets just say that
i have a creative mind
when the door is closed behind us and
when the lights are slightly dimmed

i am
that complete and
total package that
every man wishes to be
for his woman and
my goal is to
never fail at
making her smile
from ear to ear
every time she thinks of me and
every time
she speaks of me and
i want her to want me
like i want her
every day of our lives…

Breathless

if only i could dance with you
hold you in my arms
life would be a miracle
it would be
worth so much more than
it is
without you by my side

i would elevate
to a plateau so high
if only i could hold your hand
if only i
could stare into your eyes
kiss your lips
and get lost within your soul

i am a man
that needs
that W.O. beside me
that needs you
to guide me through
and release me from
the boredom of my solitude

i cannot properly breathe
without knowing that
we are not sharing the same oxygen…
that…
we are not connected…
in the way that soul mates are…
in the way that…
the one and only that God created
to stand by my side
and meant for me to share this life with
would connect to me

let me say that once again
just in case you didn't feel me

i CANNOT breathe
if you're not breathing along side of me
because
our souls have not yet mated
but i know that
God made you for me
and meant for us to connect
on that other level of love
hand in hand
and heart to heart

so i know that
He hasn't finished yet

but
patience is my virtuosity
and i will grasp it tightly
for as long as it takes
for you
to take your rightful place
deep within my world

Cheesy Love Poem

every time i see you
it's like
a new beginning
it's like
the first time our eyes met and
the first time you smiled at me and
the first time i ever approached you
before the first time you said yes

every thought
i have of you is
more intense than
the one that came before it and
i could swear that my heart stops
each time you call my name

every experience
feels brand new
because of you
and the way that you came and
brought a lamp onto my darkest days
unlocking my heart and allowing me to feel
things that i'd forgotten how to accept

i thank you
for being the one
that is willing to be there
and i hope that
together
we'll have many more
first times to come

My Recipe for Love

Ingredients:

warm heart
compassionate soul
loyal spirit
intoxicating smile
gentle demeanor
willingness to love
understanding
daunting eyes
a touch of talent
and God to top it all off

Preparation Instructions:

love me, and hold me
always be honest and
always communicate any and everything to me
so that
we will always see our way through things together

let me love you
the way you deserve to be loved and
let me hold you
when, where, and how
you need to be held

let me

rub your neck, back, and feet

when they ache and

even when they don't

as i spoil you intentionally

catering to your every little need

mix me with you and

the results shall be

a union of biblical proportions

so long

as we always

keep God

at the head of our lives

Something Beautiful (The Vows)

the moment that

the corner of my eye

caught a small glimpse of you

my system

went into shock

in awe of

the breath stealing vision

that stood right before me

my mind stuttered

flipping rapidly through words

through sentences

and through scenarios

in order to

correctly present myself

with an introduction that

would keep my composure intact

you had

an essence of elegance

draped across your demeanor and

a touch of class

spilled from within you

with each step that

you blessed the ground with

your vocals were
soothing to my ears and
your mind was
overloaded with the intelligence of
a woman who demanded that
she be taken seriously
by all that crossed her path
with knowledge so thick that
to say "God that's sexy"
would be nothing short of
an understated thought

your fragrance
had me at a standstill
frozen in the glory of
your spirit of womanhood
that was
unique
yet
natural
making parts of your anatomy glisten
while the sun accentuated your skin tone

i won you over
that day
unleashing a smile from within you that
seemed to make the world glow

and

brought nothing but happiness into my life

i've walked with you

from that day

as you have been a constant in my life

and

there is not a second

when i'm not thinking of you

not a minute

when i'm not staring at you

and not an hour inside the year

that hosts the months

formed by the days

that we have spent

by each other's side

that i don't thank God

for sending me something so beautiful

mind

body

and soul

to have with me

to support me

to love me

and to grow with me

until

i walk this earth no more

Love Defined

there is a hunger
deep inside the belly of
my broken heart
waiting to be fed with
unconditional love from
that one that quenches me
like no other has before

that one
that special lady
is like no other
she
stands taller and
looks down from
a higher pedestal than all others
for
she is my queen and
she was
personally hand crafted
by God himself and
after years of preparation and
all the obstacles
that i had to overcome
she has come to me and
i am prepared to
give her every stitch

of

the fabric

of my well being

never will she ever know love

deeper than

what lies within me and

never

will she ever

be treated with such care and

such reverence

because i for one

will always recognize her beauty

and will always feel and appreciate her strength and

from this day forward

i will hold her within the walls of my heart

showing her

every

single

day

every

single

hour

and every

single

minute that each second of our lives endure

exactly how good it is

to experience

the true definition of love

Love Restoration

slow music plays
inside my soul
each time I inhale
to exhale your name

every thought I encounter
has you embedded within it
and
i can't take two steps alone
without feeling you right beside me

i've grown so accustomed to
holding you close to me that
i go through love withdrawals
every time you're away

if it weren't for
the look of you
the touch of you
the taste of you
embroidered into
all that i claim to be
i'd fall apart
in a matter of
a single beat of my heart

the things that you've done for me
mentally...physically...and spiritually
without a second thought or
a blink of uncertainty
have restored my faith and
finally opened me up to
what a real woman is and
how to appreciate
the things that
many men take for granted

i love you
with all that my heart can withstand
and in you
these emotions will remain unshaken
as long as you
will recognize me
as your man

Putty

hold me
closely as i
inhale you slowly
sending me to
a realm of unconsciousness
placing me in a
blissful state of mind

baby you numb my senses
leaving me senseless
going in circles
trying to follow your lead

i'm entranced by your beauty…
enthralled by the mere thought of you
taken captive by your whispers and
willing to sacrifice all
just to be in your arms

you
are all that
i ever dreamed a woman could be
you're everything that
a woman should be and
you are most definitely
the woman for me

for you
i give up my will
allowing you to
take me as i am and
make me
who you want me to be…
because i can't shake you
and i'll stop short of nothing
just to be your man

My Rose

if i could
multiply this rose
giving you a dozen
it would only
duplicate the beauty
of the one you're holding at this moment
and
that would be all well and good but
the way i see it
you
are my rose
and just one of you
is sufficient enough
to smile that beautiful smile
to laugh that perfect laugh
to be…
that perfect you
that i've
fallen so much in love with
and
wish to share myself with
so
take this rose
and cherish it
just as i cherish you

and know that
you alone
are unmatched
by anything
this world has to offer

My Testament to You

as i gaze into

the hazel hue of your eyes

i'm mesmerized by

the lack of disguise

that lies within

the solid walls of your foundation

leaving my heart racing

while

bracing myself

for

the greatest love that i've ever known

and

as long as i have you

i'll never be alone

because

you have shown me that

your feelings go beyond skin

they go down to the bone deep

and it's there for me to keep

so

i'll never have to seek

another to be my lover

since…

well…

you've got me covered

yet i'm never smothered
in the depths
of all you have to give
and as long as i breathe
i'll never leave your side
this is my testament to you

Serenading

if it's your will
i am your Shakespeare
serenading you
in my garden of trust
in which your reward will be
everlasting happiness

allow me to enlighten you
show you the ways of the world
that i wish to share with you
because i feel as if
i could have something rare with you
as we do things together that most
wouldn't dare do
keeping us forever separated
from those redundant things
that cause other relationships to fail

if i may have your hand
my angel
i assure thee something magical
will take shape
in the form of an emotion
that has a greater will
than any man or woman could ever withstand

within that organ
that demands to be kept alive
that demands to have
and to keep love within its walls
and with that knowledge
you will always know
exactly how deep
my love for you goes

Can You Feel It?

can you feel
the rhythm…
the heartbeat
(if you will)

that pulse that you feel
that drives your soul insane
and almost dares you
not to move
one way or the other

that

thump…

thump…

thump…

gets into your blood stream
and it says to you in its most silent way
move…

so

you

move…

slowly at first
building momentum
until
the groove

has full control
of all your body movements
and
you have no choice
but
to just let go
and
let the moment take you
anywhere you wish to be

ahh...
now you realize
that there really is freedom
within
this thing called love
and finally
you're able
to just let go
and let it do what it do...

Music Box

to me you're like
a slow bass line
steady...constant...unwavering

your presence is necessary
and always evident
as your voice resonates beautifully
in the depths of my eardrums

when you're away
it's a sound that i miss dearly
and when you return
it only makes me appreciate you more

when i hold you i
hear the slow whine of
violins being played softly
in the midst of the wind's subtle whisper
singing a love song
dedicated to us
and this moment
that we're certain to cherish
on those days where
we reminisce on the past and

we'll remember this dance
with the ensemble of woodwinds
playing the soundtrack
that allowed us to float on air
inside of each other's minds
while my eyes smiled at yours
and we made love
on the dance floor
to the music within our hearts

The Definition

you are
the epitome of sexiness
well defined
in all aspects of
your complete and total definition
every curve that encompasses you
is perfection
at its highest level and
flaws have not a home
within the surface of your flesh

your total
and
resplendent body
is
an experience that
most men
would give all to have
do all to have and
be all to have but
there are not many who
possess the internal potential
to be appreciative of
a lady of your caliber

but without neglect i
must mention that
your mind
a super power within its own right
is so superb and superior that
one would have to stand and take note of
the sheer brilliance that escapes from you
on a level unmatched by any soul

you are the best rendition of
what God intended when
he took the first man's rib to
create the sisterhood in which you dwell
and everyday i thank Him
for you stand out above all others
who would dare call themselves
Woman

Buried Treasure

you're like
the sweetest lyrics
of my favorite love song
imprinted on my mind
every five minutes
of every hour through my day

i wake up to your melody
smiling at the fact that
i know you're with me once again

these days have been
so good that
nothing I could write
would be sufficient enough
to describe the way
you've turned my life around

you reversed
my commitment phobia
and showed me how to love again
and showed me how to trust again
and clued me in on the things
i was missing in my life

you took away my eclipse
and let the light shine through
as you unearthed the man
i thought
i'd never be again

Love in Volumes

you are

my harlequin romance

my

living love story

sending my emotions over the edge

every time you touch me

with the sound of your voice or

with your generously soft caresses and

with the beat

of your tender heart

i love

that i'm a part of

the biography of you

sharing the details of your life

throughout the pages of us

from the day i started to matter to you

until you decide

that you don't want me anymore and

i'm hoping that

we won't be a short story because

our chapters are

so in depth that

our time together should

be told in volumes

letting the world in on
an atmosphere of love
that no one has ever
bore witness to before

Can I?

can i go there with you
can i take you on a cruise
through my controlled mindset
and watch you swim through my lake of love

can i hold your hand
while you deep sea dive
into the depths
of my heart and soul

can i go there with you
if only just to support you morally and
caress you thoroughly
with my well intentioned hands

can i kiss you on your lips
while i look deep into your eyes
relaying a message of togetherness
when our five senses meet

can i..."muah" you right there
with my fingers in your hair
with the moonlight on your skin
making your beauty truly glow

can i shape and mold your love
can i spoil you with my touch
can i softly slowly and gently
take you higher than you've ever been

can i just go there with you
can i be the one for you
can i tell you i can see our son
shining brightly in your eyes

if i can…go there with you
we can spiral down a tunnel of bliss
forever caring and together sharing
a life intended for us to live
from now until the end
on a timeless journey through the stars

Connection

within
a relatively short number of breaths
taken in by you and i
i've found myself
in an abyss of sorts
trying my best not to drown
in the pool of emotions
that have quickly surrounded me

my soul has been summoned
to appear before you
to provide evidence of
the love that i have within me
that i wish to use
to spoil you in every way

i want to be
your personal caterer
leaving you
with no needs to speak about
no wants to think about
and no unanswered desires
residing in the midst of you

it's so unexplainable
the way that i feel for you and
i can't rightfully define
the details of the dreams
that i have when
thoughts of you
seem to catch me off guard but
i'm certain that this is real
and you are that part of heaven
that resides upon this earth
straight from
the loving arms of the Father Himself
in His vision
set aside by Him to be mine forever
without a thought of another
from this moment
until life…
no longer knows my name

Connection Pt. 2

whenever i look

deeply into your eyes i

can see

into the depths of your soul and

i get this feeling

this

rush

this

overwhelming warmth

that runs all over me

and it brings forth

the biggest smile that i can give

because i know

that this is genuine

and

i can only hope that

when you look at me

you feel the same way as i

you are

that magic

that

miracle called love

that only God could explain

in a personal talk with Him

for it was He that created it
and it is Him that places it in us
at the moment when
two people
that more than deserve one another
finally have each other's hearts

you make me dance
on the floor of my emotions
holding you closely and
whispering into your ear
the things
that I know you need to hear
and within those words
lie so much truth
that
nothing ever revealed unto you
outside of what we have
will ever make you
turn your back on us
because
i am you
you are me
and together...
we are one

The Reason

the reason i say i love you

is

because

i

well

i

i

feel you

i feel you

deep inside of me

in

the pit of my stomach

i feel you

running through my veins

i feel you

you've encompassed

my mind

and my soul

and repaired

that internal damage

that was done

by those who came before you

you've opened my senses
so that i can once again
see love…

i can…

hear love in your voice
whenever you call my name

i can…

smell love all over you
whenever you are near me

and…
it even lingers
whenever
we both are miles apart

i can…

taste love
on the tip of my tongue
when i inhale your presence

i can…

feel love

every time

a single thought of you passes through me

and

each time i breathe

you breathe with me and

every time i move

your spirit is at hand and

there is not a fraction of a second that

ticks upon my watch

without you holding tightly

to the reins of my thought process

everything i do

is designed to ensure your happiness

and

everything i say

is a compliment to you

and

from the inside out

i love you

and i pray to always keep you

forever by my side

for

it's your oxygen that feeds me

through the

connection that we share
and without you
my world would not exist

i feel you
lying next to me
when you're not even there and
i need you
as much as
i want you to need me
because our souls
were meant to be bonded
as it was written to be so
and by that
i shall abide
if you'll have me in your heart
the way that i have you
or
even better yet
the way that
you already
have me

Eve

one moment in time
that we'll make last forever
baby just you and i
may we always be together
holding each other close
eye contact lingering for days
never letting go
love that will surpass my dying day
i'll cry an ocean for you
if we shall ever part
there's nothing that i wouldn't do
to keep you in my heart
you are the Eve that i've longed for
and needed in my life
you are the one that i adore
my lover, my friend, my wife

Merger

you
are so deeply imbedded
within my thought process that
i can't comprehend life
without
you being a part of
all that i do

i'm so wrapped up
in the fact that
you are really here with me
and that
this is not just another phantasm
exploiting my desires to have
a good woman by my side

i look at you
and awe engulfs all of my senses
tying my tongue in knots
and wiping my mind of
the things that i want to express to you

i'm physically and mentally
overwhelmed
by the concept of

our souls accepting each other
on a level that
only the truest of hearts
could ever achieve

i dance for you
at night
happy about the fact that
when we see each other the next day
that there's a possibility
that it could be
even better than this one was

you have filled me
with so much of you and
i appreciate what we have built together and
i just never knew that
love could feel this good since…
until you came along
i'd never had it returned and
i just wanna hold you
every second that ticks
off of the minutes
in every twenty four hour cycle
of everyday i live and breathe your name

you have reached into me
and brought forth emotions that

i thought would never
see the light of day again

you walk with me
through all my triumphs and struggles
not in front of me not behind me
but right beside me
strengthening every move i make

Rhythm

can you feel that
can you feel the music
making love to your ears
while we glide across the dance floor
as if we were one entity
showing off our true emotions
through the rhythm of the dance

with every step
you put your faith in me
as i hold you tight
claiming you as mine
from now until the music in our hearts
decide to play no longer
and even after that day
our song will be remembered
and our spirits will dance again
with all the love
that we shared in the flesh

there's not enough strength
in the word devotion
that rightfully describes
what is communal between us
and there is not a creature

that stands on this earth
that could ever separate
what we have built
under an eternity
of God's gift of abundant bliss

Old Fashioned Love

i tip my hat to you
take your hand and
kiss the back of it softly and
the smooth texture of your skin
feels so good
up against my lips that
i ask humbly
if i can do it once more

i walk beside you
your hand in mine
counting each step
that we take together and
hoping that
i'll never have to stop

i open my car door for you
and as you arise from within
our eyes meet
connecting our souls subliminally
bringing a smile
across your lips and mine

i respect you
at all times and

appreciate
everything that you make me feel and
this feeling will
never be surpassed
by anyone in my life
for you are my lady
my life
and my first love

Wifey

your eyes illuminate my path
in my darkest hours
guiding me through
whatever may come

your voice sings such sweet melodies
sending me further
into the bliss of
a lullaby's intentional slumber

your lips cradle mine
with the softness
that can only be offered
by womankind

your body speaks to me
in its own language
begging me to
fulfill its every wish

and i oblige you happily
and i stand for you
and by you
forever and always your man

Rain Dance

the rain
keeps falling
making beautiful music
as if you were calling my name
i hear you whisper
with every drop that falls
come dance with me
in the earth's
liquid nourishment
let us dance
until we're drenched
with the love
that the rain has
shared with us
let us kiss
with fresh moisture upon our lips
as we get lost
in emotions of it all

As One

sitting

inside my mind

inside your soul

around our blanket of togetherness

alone

not to be bothered by those

outside our window

forever relaxed by the fact that

solitude is on our side

still not believing that

you're right here with me

my one and only

my love

my warm embrace in the midnight air

my beautiful rainbow

carrying the promise that this

my first and only love

will never fade

but will be everlasting

as our merger is set

in a foundation of trust

bound by hugs and kisses

yet forever strengthened by God

never have i ever known
someone so marvelous as this
for i know now
the true meaning of walking on air
as i have not touched the ground
since the day
we submitted to the power
that brought us together
As One Mind
One Soul
One Life

A Love Story

i met my wifey just the other day
while i was walking down the boulevard
our paths crossed
and as we exchanged smiles,
this feeling of warmth came over me
and we both stopped simultaneously
as she turns and says to me,
"so you felt that too"
i agreed that i did
and said as awkward as it is
i feel like i've known you
for quite some time
and though i know
you're still a stranger to me
somehow i just feel like
this meeting was meant to be
and i kept tossing words at her randomly
but never thought to get her number
which was stupid of me
but at the same time
i just had to test my theory
because i've never been one
that believed in destiny
so i showed up at the same place
next day same time

and there she was on a bench
lip synching one of my favorite rhymes

standing behind her i cleared my throat
"ahem, miss is this seat taken"
she smiled from ear to ear
then said "you're late"
"i've been here waiting"
so i sat down next to her
as i have each day that's followed
suddenly i'm not alone
and i can't describe the feeling
there's a magic that's unequalled
in the way we fellowship
nothing's ever been this easy
i'm afraid this dream will end
but i hope this moment
stays within my grasp

Acquaintance

i cleared my throat
to get your attention
as rude as it may seem
i panicked
and all other means of communication
ceased to exist in my world

when i saw you
walking that walk
that you so obviously made your own
i just had to know
if there was more to you
than your strut
your curves
and that pause flash smile of yours

i had to be sure that
your intelligence was up to par
and that
your demeanor was tolerable
and
if you believed
like i believed
that God had a hand
in our so-called chance meeting

because if not for Him
i would not have had
the courage to call you over...

my confidence received a sudden boost
and now i'm standing
face to face with you
wanting to know
your life's story
so that i may add
a chapter of my own
then wishing i could
skip to the end
just to see if i was still there

i see so much of you
through your eyes
and i just wish to be at least
a small contributor to the wellness of your being
i want to be beneficiary
to the smile across your lips
i want
to be the I
in the middle of your happiness
as you become
the U in my soul

i gather roses
to celebrate
and honor your existence
wishing, no praying
for longevity
in the life we've started
on this day
together
on the path
that we will walk hand in hand

The Reality of You

i'm breathless
lost in those eyes of yours that
showed me the contents of your soul
on the day that we met

the reality of you
has finally settled in and
i can see and feel
exactly what you mean to me

the reality of you
is that
i am now complete
because
you are that missing piece of me
that i sought after
in the midst of the ones
that i
never completely connected with

you are
my missing rib
and until this moment
nothing in this world
has ever fit me so perfectly

because
you've been here
through everything
and have
been my source of comfort
every step of the way

My Life's, One Love

you are my
real-time queen
so divine
as you walk and talk with me
guiding me through
all things hand in hand
inhaling your beauty
every time i'm near you
with a clear view
of the most splendid gift
God ever parted with
and bestowed unto me

baby

how your name
rolls off of my tongue
like the sweetest nectar
of the fruits
that mother nature provides
making me smile
each time
i have the privilege to speak it

sweet lady

the definition of you
could only be pure
for you are that angel
that i hold near
and cherish always
and hope to keep by my side
as long as you wish
for me to be your man

My Personal Eve

my intimate gravitational pull
draws you closer and closer to me
come as you are this time around
let me be your personal day spa and
treat you to the luxurious life you crave
money is of no necessity when love is the payment's form
i wanna massage you, undress you, wine you, and spit-shine you
so that all men will turn heads when they see you on my arm
not to sound like you're my trophy because you know you're so much more
just wanna show the world the pride i have for you every chance i get
my comfort level rises when i have you here with me
you are my den of happiness and without you i'm a mess
you're the dawn that starts my every day
so content i am without the desolation of loneliness
you feed my starving soul with love's pure intent
as i contemplate the life we share, a smile comes from within
so spectacular a union could only exist through the hand of God
for He took away my rib for you to be here by my side
my lady, my personal eve for me to always have and hold
my sun, my rain, my bad and good, together eternally

Forever

i am standing
in the midst of
the perfect moment
with
the perfect woman
right here in front of me

as i
hold your hand
and look into your eyes
know that
these vows
are coming
straight from the heart of God
through me
to
deliver you
from all things in your past
up until the moment
that you knew
that i'd be yours forever

Dear Lady

dear lady
i've never felt
more calm and
more complete
than right now at this moment

i can
hear
speak
and think clearly
because i know that
with you
things in my life
will never go wrong again

i've prayed
for this moment
over and over again
playing out this scenario
repeatedly inside my mind

not even in my imagination
have i seen such beauty
such poise
and

it's all for me

and

i'm all for you

i take you now

to be my forever

to

have you

to

keep you

to

love you

for an eternity

underneath the hand of God

My Angel

as i stand before you…
our friends…
and our family
i'm making a promise to you
and to God that
you are
and will be
my one and only
from this moment forth

it was
divine intervention
the day that we met and
my smile
has been present
ever since that moment

you've touched a spot
beneath my heart that
reaches
all the way
down to my soul

you are
the reason i breathe

you have shown me
how to show my true self
to you

on this day
i am satisfied
and i am gracious
because i know
that my angel
is right here
holding my hand

Love Jonz

to catch a glimpse of the starry night
through the wonders of your eyes
would be
so astounding
surrounding me with the love of your internal organ
that always shares more than it has to give

if only i could live within the thought of us
meaning you me and God
in a simple word that means so much
when spoken behind a synopsis of truth
engaging us both and holding us in a nether realm of
lustful intentions directed from me to you eternally

let others watch and learn as we
share our souls with those who don't know
the way love is supposed to go
misguided by what lies below the beltline
drawn into numerous stop and go scenarios

and as our days fall by the wayside
let us forever have no regrets
on the inside
of our circle of felicity ensuring the longevity
of what we already know will come to be
the greatest ardency we will have ever known

Anticipation

let me

whisper something to you

softly

and slowly

in order to

jump start your imagination and

get your juices flowing once again

let me

walk around you in circles

inhaling your

hypnotic fragrance

allowing myself

to become intoxicated by your scent

as i

kiss you on your neck and

run my fingers

down

the side of your face and

down the small of your back

i can see

just how much

you want this to happen

i can tell by

the anticipation in your quivering lips

and

how you tense up

with

every

single

touch

that i make

this is

so crucial

and

it is

the moment that we've both

been anxiously waiting for

and

i can feel

your excitement

coming from your pores

quickening

with each moment that passes

just waiting for me to say…

turn off the lights

and let the honeymoon begin